Purple Ronnie's

Little Thoughts about

Christmas

by Purple Ronnie

First published 2004 by Boxtree
an imprint of PanMacmillan Publishers Ltd
20 New Wharf Road
London N1 9RR

www.panmacmillan.com

Associated companies throughout the world

ISBN 0 7522 2561 8

9 8 7 6 5 4 3 2 1

A CIP catalogue record for this book is
available from the British Library

Text by Giles Andreae
Illustrations by Janet Cronin
Printed and Bound in Hong Kong

Happy Christmas!

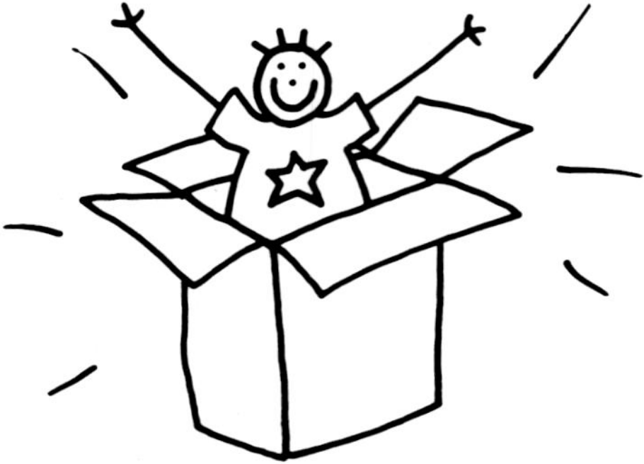

a poem to say

Happy Christmas

I've filled this special
yuletide book

With loads of festive cheer

For a very Merry Christmas

And a fabulous New Year!

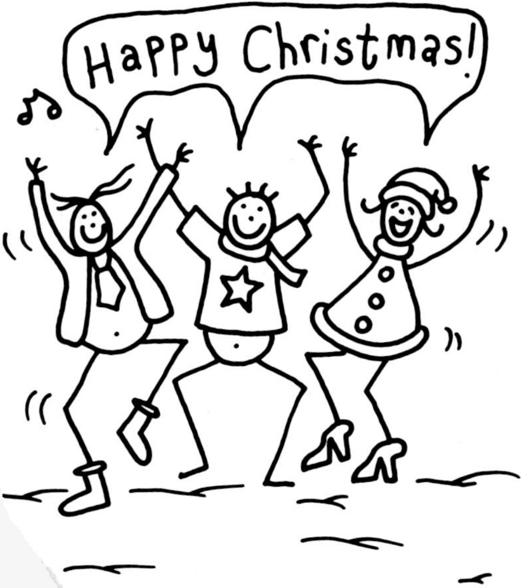
Happy Christmas!

Christmas Presents

Sometimes it's hard pretending that giant home-made jumpers are just what you've always wanted

a poem about
Reindeer

I waved at Santa's
reindeer
When I saw them in the
sky
But when they saw me
looking up
They did one in my eye!

The Office Party

At the office party,
you must always
remember to leave a
photocopy of your bum
on the boss's desk

a poem about

Carol Singing

We go off collecting
To fill up our tin
We bellow so loudly
And make such a din
That the people we sing to
Just kneel down and pray
And give loads of money
To send us away!

Dieting

Christmas is a fab excuse to eat loads of treats cos you can always pretend to yourself that you're going on a massive diet straight afterwards!

a poem about

The Queen's Speech

When the Queen starts
reading out
Her special Christmas speech

All the grown-ups fall
asleep

And all the children
screech!

Brussels Sprouts

Beware - everyone knows that brussels sprouts make you do incredibly stinky farts

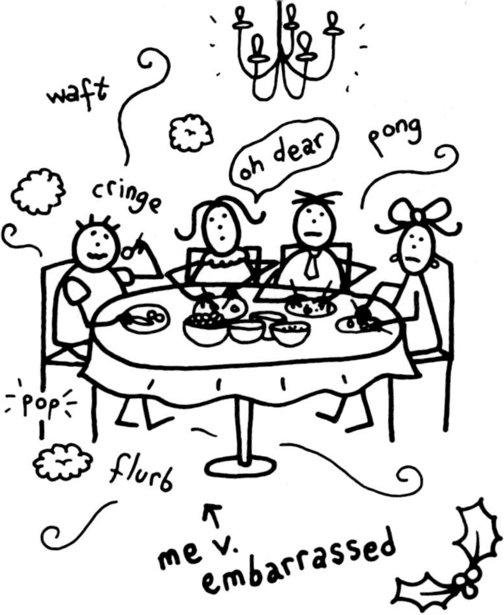
waft
oh dear
pong
cringe
pop
flurb
me v.
embarrassed

a poem about
Slobbing Out

It's great slobbing out over
Christmas
And totally stuffing your belly
Then lying flat out on the
sofa
To watch a great movie
on telly !

Big Wobbly Aunties

Watch out for big wobbly aunties at Christmas who come to give you slobbery-lipped kisses

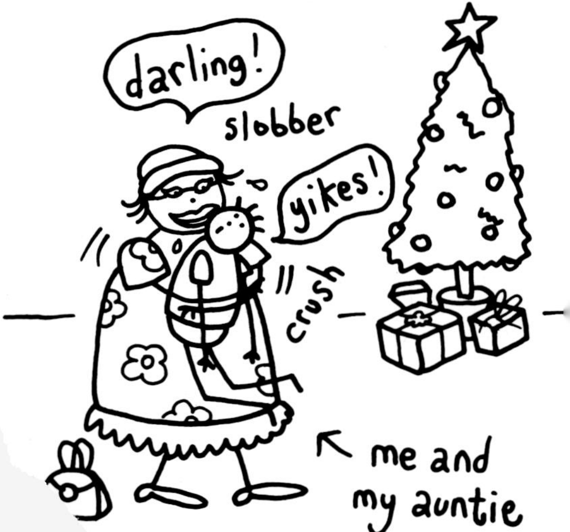
darling!
slobber
yikes!
crush
me and my auntie

a poem about

Santa

Santa comes just once a
year
So why not make him merry
With a couple of hundred
pints of beer
Instead of a thimble of
sher

Families

Families love nothing better than getting together at Christmas for a few drinks too many and a great big row!

a poem about my
Christmas Present

I tried to find a present
To make you think of me
Something very special
But for less than 20p

20p

Happy Christmas!
um...thank you
beam
whiff
my favouritest old t-shirt

Mistletoe

Mistletoe is a great excuse to get your mitts on the person you've fancied all year

a poem about a

Christmas Kiss

When I close my eyes
and dream
My dreams go just like this
I'm giving you the most
delicious
Scrumptious Christmas
Kiss!

Christmas Crackers

How come Christmas crackers are full of such awful jokes and useless toys, but they're still so much fun ?!

a poem about
Santa's List

I wrote a note to Santa
For loads of booze and chocs
But instead he gave
               me hankies
And horrid pairs of socks!

Hangovers

By the time Christmas comes, most people are so hung over that they wish it would go away again very quickly!

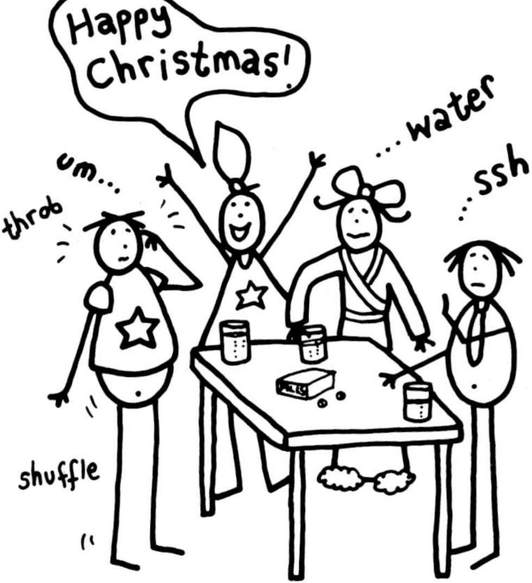
Happy Christmas!
um...
throb
...water
...ssh
shuffle

a poem about
Christmas Baubles

My girlfriend sweetly
asked me

To decorate the tree

So I went and got my
baubles out

For all the world to
see!

Mince Pies

Whether you like them or not, your Mum always tries to stuff you full of too many mince pies

a poem about a

Pissed Christmas

It's time to go crazy at
Christmas
But try not to utterly
spoil it
By ending up totally pissed
in the lav
With your head hanging
over the toilet!

a poem to say

Merry Christmas

I wish you a Merry
Christmas
And a happy New Year
With masses of
chocolate
And telly and beer!